The Time of
The Shining Rocks

A Time-Travel Adventure
Into Upper Michigan History

By
Ragene Henry

This book is dedicated to Mr. Dale Blichman,
my eleventh grade English teacher,
who was the first to believe that I was a writer.

ISBN # 0-9670743-0-4

Cover Art by Kathy Waters

The Time of The Shining Rocks

Chapter 1

From the last seat in the corner Libby watched the second hand jump on the big round classroom clock. It didn't glide from one short black line to the next. It hopped. Each time it hopped Libby put one finger down on her desk. When she got to the last finger she put a tally mark on her paper.

Tally marks marched across five rows of her notebook page and still Mrs. Maxim talked on and on.

Every now and then one of Mrs. Maxim's words got through the hums and rustles and clock jumping and finger plopping. "Michigan Week......bla bla bla...Social Studies....bla bla bla.....two page written report....bla bla bla....Native Americans......bla bla bla......discovery....."

I wish Mrs. M. would make a discovery — that it's recess time, Libby thought.

Snap! The lead in her pencil broke. She had pressed too hard on the last tally mark. But it just made her so mad. Didn't Mrs. Maxim know it was May? Hadn't she counted, like Libby had, so she'd know that there were only seventeen days left of school? This was going to spoil her plan. She was all set to shut down her school-work motor. After chugging up the hard hill of school all year, she was ready to coast downhill until the last day.

Chill out. Take it easy. Relax. Set the cruise control. Now Mrs. Maxim comes along with this big assignment that was going to count for triple grades in Social Studies and Language Arts. Drat!

Then two of her teacher's words shouted out at Libby. "Field trip." She shook her head to clear everything else out and concentrated on what Mrs. Maxim was saying.

". . . field trip. Tomorrow. We're going to take a bus and go to a park in the town of Negaunee. It will be about a half hour bus ride. We are each going to pack a bag lunch. I'll bring lemonade for everyone. We'll have a picnic lunch there. After lunch we will go to the Marquette County Historical Society Museum and see the displays on mining history and the Ojibwa, the native tribe of Upper Michigan."

Some of the kids shouted, "Yea!" or "All right!"

Mrs. Maxim smiled. "But...." She held up her finger and waited for their attention again. "But, the picnic isn't the important part. This is a Social Studies field trip. It goes along with the Native American unit we've been studying and with Michigan history month."

Several kids groaned. Mrs. Maxim ignored them. "We're going to Miners' Park in Negaunee because there is a monument there marking the spot where an Ojibwa chief named Marji Gesick led the white men to the discovery of iron ore and the beginning of the mining industry we have today. You know how important the mines are. Many of your parents and grandparents have worked in the mines. You know the iron mines of the Marquette Range are one of the biggest employers in our area."

Heads nodded around the room. Not Libby's. Her dad lived in Minnesota and her mom's job was baby-sitting other people's kids. She didn't really know what her grandparents' jobs had been. They were retired now.

Mrs. Maxim flapped a stack of yellow papers in the air. "Here are your permission slips. Each of you has to bring one home, get it signed by a parent, and bring it back to school tomorrow. Don't forget or you won't be able to go on our trip."

Mrs. M. didn't have to worry about Libby forgetting. A picnic. A bus ride that would take at least an hour (both ways together). Looking at a monument. Going to a museum. She bet they'd miss nearly the whole school day, especially if kids thought of lots of questions to ask.

Libby started thinking up questions. She'd write them all down so she wouldn't forget. She'd put the list in her lunch bag.

As Mrs. Maxim passed the papers out Libby dug in her desk for her little blue pencil sharpener. She stuck her pencil into the hole and started turning it. She watched the curled shavings with the yellow zigzag edges crawl out of the sharpener blade. Maybe she could break her record for the longest shaving. While she twirled the pencil she began to plan what she'd fix for her picnic lunch. A peanut butter and jelly sandwich, some Oreo cookies, some grapes if the daycare kids hadn't eaten them up. Her hand kept going round and round with the pencil. She stopped thinking about lunch and looked down at the sapphire birthstone ring sparkling from her third finger. It was her most favorite possession, a gift sent from Grandma Swanson all the way from Arizona. She loved how it sparkled when she wiggled her fingers, shooting off blue and silver stars into the air.

Then she noticed how close her fingers were getting to the sharpener. Drat! She had turned her new ten inch pencil into a four inch stub. She made a mad bear face.

3

Then she shrugged her shoulders. Oh, well, it was too late now.

Should she bring an apple? Would Mom buy her a small bag of potato chips? How many questions could she write with her short pencil to keep Mrs. M. talking and keep the bus from returning them to school too soon? Maybe they would be gone long enough so they wouldn't have to take their math test. She certainly hoped so.

Chapter 2

"Did you bring lunch for the whole class?" Libby's best friend Samantha asked the next morning.

"No. It was the only size bag I could find," Libby answered, making a lizard face at the Econo-Valu Supermarket bag she carried. "Besides, my mother made me take a sweatshirt so I put that in, too. And my list of questions." She didn't say that she'd only been able to think of two questions so far.

"Hurry up," Samantha urged as they approached the door to Room 21.

It was loud in Room 21 this morning. Kids chattered excitedly about the field trip, argued about who was going to sit with whom on the bus, and compared bag lunches. Mrs. Maxim was trying to gather permission slips, take attendance, and keep order, but she was not having an easy time.

Finally she went to her desk, pulled out her recess whistle, and blew a long shrill note. The kids quieted down. "Everyone at your seats. We are not going anywhere until we take care of business and get organized."

"Organized - shnorganized," Libby grumbled. Mrs. M. was big on being organized.

Mrs. Maxim put the whistle chain around her neck and

began organizing the class. At last it was time to line up to go outside and get on the bus. "We'll line up by being able to tell a fact about Michigan history," she said, smiling like she'd just had the world's most brilliant idea.

"History - twistory," Libby griped.

Nathan Westlake's hand flew into the air first, as usual. Mrs. Maxim called on him.

"Michigan was the 26th state to become part of the United States," he said in his you-know-I'm-the-smartest-kid-in-the-class voice.

"Correct, Nathan." Mrs. Maxim smiled at him. "You may line up." Libby made a twitchy rabbit face at Nathan Westlake when he passed her desk. Big show off, fat brain, she thought.

Corey Stebbens was next. "The capital of Michigan is Lansing." He got to line up.

Libby tried to think of a history fact. But the only history thing that popped into her mind was Paul Revere's ride and she knew that was during the Revolutionary War and had nothing to do with Michigan. In fact, there wasn't even such a thing as Michigan during the Revolutionary War, was there? Could she say that? Could she say there was no state of Michigan at the time Paul Revere rode around shouting about the British coming? She chewed her fingernail while she thought. She knew there were some kids who would never get a fact and finally Mrs. M. would give up and tell them all to join the end of the line so they could get going on the field trip. They'd have the last choice of bus seats. They'd have to sit in front with the teacher and the bus driver and Trisha's mom who was coming along to help.

Libby did not want to be one of them.

Two more kids gave facts. They were using up all the

good ideas. Why couldn't she think of anything?

Samantha got called next. She said, "The state bird of Michigan is the robin." She got to line up. As she passed Libby's desk she made a sign with her hand, palm up, raising it up, up, up, as if she were saying, "Come on, Lib, get your hand up so we can sit together."

And then suddenly, pop, a fact from yesterday bounced into Libby's mind. She waved her hand and Mrs. Maxim called her name. "Iron ore was discovered by an Indian chief named Marching Geeses."

Giggles. Snorting sounds behind her. Oh, my gosh, she must have messed it up. She could feel hot redness creeping up her neck and flooding her cheeks.

Mrs. M. didn't laugh but she smiled loudly. "Close, Libby. It was Chief Marji Gesick. Say it with me. Mar—jee Ghee—sick."

Libby repeated it, "Mar—jee Ghee-sick."

"You may line up."

She was glad that close was good enough today. She snatched up her big grocery bag and got in line just behind Samantha who grabbed her hand in a squeeze.

Soon Mrs. Maxim told the rest of the class to line up and they followed her down the hall, out the big double doors, and onto bus 92B. Libby and Samantha found a seat in the second from the back row. Perfect.

The bus doors closed with a whoosh and the motor grumbled and belched. Finally the bus began rolling across the parking lot. The kids started singing. " This is the song that never ends. It goes on and on, my friends. Some people started singing it not knowing what it was, and now continue singing it forever just because........This is the song that never ends. It goes on and on......,"

7

Chapter 3

Mrs. Maxim stood up in the aisle at the front of the bus. "Welcome to Iron Town, USA," she said.

"What? I thought we were going to Negaunee," shouted Jeff Small. Libby was thinking the same thing.

"We are in Negaunee. Iron Town, USA is Negaunee's nick-name, because iron ore was first discovered here," Mrs. Maxim explained.

"Duh!" Samantha said, disgusted. "Doesn't he know that's the whole reason we're coming on this field trip today? Mrs. Maxim explained it all yesterday."

Libby was glad she hadn't said anything. She looked out the window as the bus slowed and turned off the highway. "There's the park," she said to Samantha. And look, there's the stone monument."

Miners' park was small, about the size of a city block, but shaped like a triangle drawn by a kindergartner. Scattered maple trees shaded a few picnic tables. A rusty old iron ore railroad car, a tiny log cabin the size of a playhouse, and two basketball courts decorated the park. Best of all, Libby spied a play yard, one of those neat ones with slides and climbing ropes and a swinging bridge. And, of course, there was the monument.

Libby could hardly wait to get to the swinging bridge.

She hoped she could catch Nathan Westlake on it and give him a swing that would send him flying so he'd land on his smart old head.

But it was almost like Mrs. Maxim could read her mind. "Now, class," she said, "before you go off to play and have lunch we're going to investigate the monument and learn some local history. So, when you get off the bus go directly to the monument."

"Investigate - shimestigate," Libby thought. Grown ups. They always make you do the bad stuff before you can get to the good stuff, like eating your vegetables before you get dessert, or doing your homework before you watch TV.

The kids tumbled off the bus and ran to the base of the monument. It looked much bigger when you got right up to it. Libby had to tip her head way back to see the top of it.

The monument was shaped like a pyramid and built of stones piled on top of each other and cemented in. The stones were different colors and sizes. Some had interesting orangey-brown stripes and swirls. Some sparkled silvery black like crumpled tin foil. Some were plain brown or black. Libby figured some of them were iron ore. Which ones?

In the middle of the side of the pyramid where Libby and Samantha stood rested a large bronze plaque with lots of writing on it.   Libby tried to read it but she didn't know some of the words. It didn't matter. She knew Mrs. Maxim would read it to them.

"This is a State of Michigan Historic Marker," Mrs. Maxim explained. "It was put here so people would know that something important happened here. Let's read it and see." She began to read the words on the plaque in a loud, dramatic voice.

" ' This monument was erected by the Jackson Iron Co. in October 1904, to mark the first discovery of iron ore in the Lake Superior region. The exact spot is 300 feet North Easterly from this monument, to an iron post. The ore was found under the roots of a fallen pine tree, in June 1845, by Marji Gesick, a chief of the Chippewa tribe of Indians. The land was secured by a mining "permit" and the property subsequently developed by the Jackson Mining Company, organized July 23, 1845.'

"Here's what that means," she explained in her teacher voice. "The white men were exploring for minerals. They knew there was iron ore around here somewhere because they had heard about William A. Burt's findings from the year before. Mr. Burt had been mapping the area into pieces of land that settlers could buy. Suddenly his magnetic compass began to go crazy, spinning and jumping around instead of pointing north."

"That's not possible," said Nathan Westlake. "The needle on a compass always points north. My scout leader said so."

"Well, that's true... but not in this case. And that's what was so strange. Mr. Burt and his men had never seen a compass act like that. So they started to look around, trying to find out what was causing the compass to go crazy. They found some rocks sticking out of the side of a hill that were causing it. What do you think those rocks were?"

"Iron ore?" Samantha volunteered.

"That's right. The rocks were actually chunks of magnetic iron ore. But Mr. Burt didn't make a big deal of it. He didn't even put it on his maps. All he was interested in was finishing his survey so settlers could buy the land and build farms and towns on it.

"Jeffrey! Get back here right this minute!" Even though he was behind her, Mrs. Maxim had noticed Jeff Small sneaking off toward the play yard. Maybe it was true, Libby thought. Maybe Mrs. Maxim did have eyes in the back of her head, hidden by her thick curly black hair.

"So," Mrs. Maxim continued, "these mining explorers knew there was iron ore somewhere, but they couldn't find exactly where. They were ready to give up. Just in time they met a local Ojibwa chief named Marji Gesick. He knew where the shining dark ore could be found. So he led them to it."

"Mrs. Maxim?" It was Nathan Westlake again. "How come you say it was an Ojibwa chief and the plaque says he was a Chippewa?"

"Wow! You have really been paying attention, Nathan." Mrs. Maxim turned her hundred watt smile on him. Libby stuck her finger in her mouth and made a barf face.

"Lots of people have tried to answer that question. From what I've read, both words are names for the same tribe. When these Native Americans talk about themselves they use the name Ojibwa. When white people talked about them they used the name Chippewa."

Libby understood that. When she talked about herself she used the name Libby. When other people, especially people who didn't know her well, talked about her, they used her official name, Elizabeth. She smiled at Mrs. Maxim and nodded her head up and down so Mrs. Maxim could see that she understood.

Mrs. Maxim continued. "Legend says that Marji Gesick led them to the roots of a large pine tree that had fallen over, lifting up the ground and showing chunks of iron ore.

12

But no one knows if that's really true or just a legend or story.

"Jeffrey!" Mrs. Maxim shrieked. "Get down off those rocks. If I say your name once more you are going to wait in the bus until we leave.

"Anyway," she took a deep breath and continued. "These men made a careful map and then went back to lower Michigan to get a permit, or permission, to start an iron mine. They called their company The Jackson Mining Company because they were from the city of Jackson, Michigan. In 1845 they started mining and since that time more than forty eight billion dollars worth of iron ore has been mined in the area. That's forty eight followed by nine zeros! And it's forty seven billion dollars more than all the gold in the California Gold Rush."

"Did they all get rich?" someone asked.

"I don't know if those explorers got rich from it, but I know Marji Gesick didn't. They gave him a few shares of mining stock but he never collected any money. He died poor."

"No fair!" yelled several kids.

"He got ripped off!" said Nathan Westlake.

"If I was him I'd have been REAL mad," said Samantha.

"I'd have sued those guys for a million dollars," said Libby. She made her most ferocious pit bull face.

Chapter 4

From the backside of the monument came Nathan Westlake's voice. "Mrs. Maxim! There's another plaque back here that says this monument was taken apart and moved here from its original site."

All the kids ran around to the other side of the monument. All except Libby and Samantha whose arm Libby clutched. "Big show off," Libby grumbled, making a fierce wolverine face. Too late she remembered that the wolverine was Michigan's state animal. "He probably won't even get in trouble for being on the wrong side."

"Yeah, probably," Samantha agreed.

They could hear Mrs. Maxim's voice. "Good detective work, Nathan." Libby and Samantha both stuck their fingers toward their open mouths making retching sounds before they burst into giggles.

Mrs. Maxim came marching back around to their side, kids straggling after her. "So the actual site........" Mrs. Maxim looked around. Her forehead wrinkled while she figured it out. She pointed across the highway toward downtown Negaunee. "Actually, it's about a mile and a half that way where Marji Gesick led them. But, don't forget, it looked a whole lot different here in 1845. There were no towns, not even Marquette, only forests, Native

American villages and hunting grounds."

Libby squinted her eyes and tried to see beyond the houses and gas stations and banks to what it must have looked like when this was all forests of tall trees where wild animals and only a few Native Americans wandered. She thought it must have been awesome.

"Okay, kids, take a look around. Study the monument. Think about what happened and how it affected the history of Upper Michigan. Then you can go play and I'll set up the lemonade for lunch at that picnic table. Stay inside the park and out of the streets."

Mrs. M. had already turned her back and was walking toward the picnic table when Libby remembered her list of questions. Oh well, she could ask them after lunch. Besides that gave her time to think of more. And questions about what happened and about Marji Gesick and how he felt were beginning to poke at her brain.

As the rest of the kids ran off to the play yard or the basketball courts Libby grabbed Samantha's hand and pulled her around all four sides of the monument studying the shapes and sizes and colors of the rocks. She stared up at the monument so long that her neck started to hurt. On the west side of the monument one rock really interested her. It was cemented in just above the plaque. It was shaped like a flower pot and was a shiny, shiny silvery color. She wanted to touch it. It looked as if the silvery stuff would rub off on her fingers like glitter.

She set her lunch bag down on the ground beside the monument. "Give me a boost," she said to Samantha. "I want to touch that shiny one up there. Do you think it's iron ore like the shining rocks Marji Gesick found?"

"Uh-uh." Samantha shook her head. "We'll get in trouble."

"For once in your life don't be such a goody-goody," Libby coaxed. She knew that if there was one thing Samantha hated it was being called a goody-goody. "Come on. Mrs. Maxim will never notice us over here. She'll be too busy making sure no one gets pushed off the bridge or hit in the head with a swing or something. Now, boost me up."

Samantha gave her a skeptical look but she laced her fingers together into a stirrup. Libby put her foot into Samantha's hands and hoisted herself up, grabbing onto the faces of rocks that stuck out even a little bit. She got her other foot up onto the edge of a rock. She reached as far as she could, stretching and wiggling her fingers. But she was just barely short of the rock.

"Higher. Boost me higher," she called down to Samantha. Samantha grunted and strained to raise her arms. Finally Libby's fingers touched the silvery stone. "I got it!" she yelled.

She looked up and saw her sapphire birthstone ring and the silvery stone shining together. Sparkling. Dancing in the sunlight. Shooting blue and silver stars.

"I can't hold you much longer," Samantha called. She grumbled, "I never thought you'd get so interested in anything about history."

The shafts of light bursting in Libby's eyes from the ring and the rock were almost blinding her. "Michigan-swishigan, history-twistory, Spark-ily park-ily," she chanted, ready to come down.

But something strange began happening. The lights started to dance dizzily in her eyes while the rest of the world faded away. She felt weird, light-headed. Out of control. It felt as if some strange and powerful magnetic force was drawing her in, stretching her toward the sparkling lights inside the shining rock. It pulled at her until her hand, then her arm seemed to disappear into the darkness at the heart of the rock. She took a big shuddering breath as the magnetic force pulled her away from all she knew. She was inside darkness, a darkness as black as a witch's cave. She was falling, falling, into a black tunnel with a brilliant silvery light at its center, blinding her.

Chapter 5

"Ow!" Libby's head hurt. Her back hurt. Her elbows hurt. What was she doing lying on the cold hard ground? Oh, yeah, a weird, dizzy, pulling feeling had come over her. She must have fallen off the monument. She felt like Humpty-Dumpty. But when she checked she was still all together. Just sore. But why was it dark? It was supposed to be lunch time.

Libby sat up and pressed her fingers to the sore spot on the back of her head. "Double ow!"

As the dizziness in her head cleared, Libby looked around her. No Samantha. No kids. No monument. No park. No bus. Only the dark shadowy shapes of tall trees and the brown pad of dry leaves and pine needles where she sat. Where was everybody?

It was very dark, darker than it had been at 10:00 last Halloween night, the latest Libby had ever been outside alone. No street lights. No houses. Nothing. Just darkness and tall trees.

"Where in the world am I?" she wondered. Fear began to nibble at her backbone. She was alone, at night, in a forest. She had no idea where she was. How had she gotten there? How could she find her way home?

She began to hear noises creeping in on her from all

directions. Skittering, scary noises. Leaves rustling, she told herself. Crickets chirping. No bears. Absolutely no bears. She heard a distant howl. Shivering, she wrapped her arms around her knees and tried to think.

She couldn't just sit here all night. But she had no idea what to do. If she could get up the courage to move, which direction should she try? Cautiously she stood up and turned slowly in a circle. There. Through the thick wavery wall of trees she could see a faint light dancing. A light? A house maybe? She turned toward it.

Another howl sounded deep in the forest behind her. She crossed her arms and held onto herself tightly. Biting down on her lower lip, she tried not to cry. She felt help-less in the darkness. She couldn't even tell if there was a moon. The trees were too tall and thick to see the moon even if it were up there.

"Ok, Libby, don't panic. Get a grip on yourself. You've got to get out of here," she said to herself in a whisper. "You can do it. Come on. It's probably just a bad dream. Let's go," she told herself. Stiffly she began making her way, stumbling through the darkness toward the faint flickering light far ahead.

She seemed to be on some sort of path. The dirt was flattened and hard from many feet, or hooves, ...or paws, she reminded herself with a shudder. Close on either side of the path the trees and bushes crowded in, slapping her arms and legs. A couple of times she tripped over roots but regained her balance and started off again, drawn like a moth toward the dancing light.

She was so tired. And so hungry. It was way past lunch time. And she was cold. She wished she had taken her sweatshirt out of her lunch bag. She wished she had her lunch bag right now. She wanted to eat and be warm and sleep.

Just when she felt she couldn't walk another step, the light seemed to get bigger and brighter. She heard voices. They were muffled and not understandable. They had to be human voices. Bears would sound like hoarse growls, wouldn't they? She made her tired legs move faster.

Then suddenly the trees and bushes ended. She found herself at the edge of a clearing looking at a strange and awesome sight.

In the middle of the clearing a campfire burned, tossing crackly sparks high into the air. That must have been the dancing light I saw, she thought. Behind the fire the dark ripples of a lake shone with silvery tips where the moonlight glanced. The moon itself hung over high hills that surrounded the lake on all sides except this one. To Libby the hills surrounding the lake looked like a large cupped hand holding water to drink. Here, on the wrist side, the clearing swept down to the lake and became a beach where two canoes rested half in and half out of the water.

On both sides of the campfire Libby saw the strange huddled shapes of rounded tents or huts. But the strangest sight of all was the people who sat around the campfire. They didn't look like any campers she'd ever seen.

A few were scraggly, bearded men dressed in dark old-fashioned clothes and tall boots.

The others seemed to Libby to be Indians. There were only a few of them and they were all men, dressed in pale brown tunics and pants of buckskin. Instead of boots, they wore tall moccasins that tied just below their knees. Dark, shoulder length hair gleamed in the firelight. One man, in the center, wore a bright red woolen jacket over his buckskins. He spoke in a deep voice. The others quieted and listened when he spoke. He lifted a long smoking pipe, took a deep breath of the tobacco and passed the pipe to the bearded white man next to him.

What is this, some kind of state park where they wear costumes and act out scenes from the past? That was the only explanation that made sense to Libby.

A voice came out of the darkness behind her. Libby felt like she nearly jumped right out of her skin at the sound. "Who are you? What do you do here?" the voice asked.

Just what I've been wondering, Libby thought, but she was too startled to speak. She whirled and saw a girl standing in the shadows beside her, only an arm's length away. The girl looked a little older and taller than Libby. She was dressed in a long, shapeless buckskin dress. Her dark hair hung over her shoulder in one thick glossy braid. She stared steadily at Libby.

"Geez, you scared me to death," Libby said. She tried to get her heartbeat under control. "How did you sneak up on me? Where'd you come from? Who are you?"

"I walk soft," the girl said in a low musical voice. "Come from there." She lifted an arm and pointed toward the huts near the fire. She repeated her questions, "Who are you? What do you do here?"

"I'm Libby Larson. I'm lost. I was in the forest and I saw a light so I followed it."

The girl looked at Libby suspiciously for a long moment. Then she seemed to decide something. She nodded once and said proudly, pointing to her own chest, "Me, Sailing With The Wind. White man name Charlotte, daughter of Marji Gesick."

Chapter 6

"Marji Gesick?"

"Yes." The girl nodded. "My father." She pointed at the group of men by the fire. Her finger jabbed directly toward the man in the red jacket.

"But...." Libby looked from the girl to the group of men at the fire, then back to the girl again. The girl, Charlotte, waited patiently. Libby was so confused. It couldn't be the same Marji Gesick, could it?"

"But," she searched her brain, trying to remember what the plaques on the monument had said. "But Marji Gesick lived in the 1800s."

"Yes. White man say year is 1845," Charlotte replied with a look that wondered why Libby didn't know what year it was.

"1845? But that's not possible. It's supposed to be lunch time more than a hundred and fifty years after that."

Now the girl looked at her like she was crazy. Of course she must seem crazy. It was a crazy thing to say. And it was even crazier if it was true. She had to find out more. "Charlotte, who are those men with your father?"

Charlotte made a snorting sound through her nose. "Ha!" she said with disdain. "White men come many weeks' journey. Look for shining rocks. They call iron." She shook her head and stretched her lips in a look of scorn. "They not find. Beg father help them. My father great man. He know earth; share earth. When sun come up he show way to shining rocks."

Libby could scarcely believe what she was hearing. It was the same Marji Gesick that Mrs. Maxim had talked about! The same one on the monument. The one who led the mining explorers to the discovery of iron ore in 1845. And she was here. She would see it happen in the morning.

But how could that be? Libby's mind raced with possibilities. She must have somehow traveled back in time. Maybe she stepped through a time portal like Hannah in The Devil's Arithmetic, a book Mrs. Maxim had read to the class.

She tried to remember what had happened. The class was at Miners' Park on a field trip to learn about Marji Gesick and the iron ore discovery. Samantha had given her a boost so she could reach the sparkly silvery rock high up on the side of the monument. The sun had glinted off the rock and her birthstone ring, stabbing into her eyes so she had to squint them shut. Samantha said something. She said something. Then she got dizzy and a force like a magnet had pulled at her. Blinding lights and blackness had closed around her. She had fainted or something, and when she woke up....

"Oh, my gosh," she said in an awed voice. When she woke up on the ground it was 1845. It didn't seem possible. Could it be a dream? She reached out and touched the buckskin sleeve and then the shining black braid of the girl beside her. Charlotte was real. And if Charlotte was real, then Marji Gesick and the mining men must be real, too. Oh, boy, was she going to have a social studies story to give to Mrs. Maxim when she got back. That is, if she could get back to her own time.

Charlotte had been watching the men at the fire but when Libby touched her she turned. "Lost?" she asked. "Where come from?"

Libby tried to think. It was too complicated to explain. There were no towns, just native villages in 1845. How could she explain to Charlotte where she had come from? She shook her head slowly, realizing that she could think of nothing to say.

"Come. I take you to wigwam of father. You stay. After he show shining rocks we go home to Carp River, take you. Father help you find way to family." She began walking toward the hut closest to the fire. Libby followed her.

Inside the hut it was warm and sweet smelling. A small flame glowed on an oily surface inside a clay bowl. Animal furs covered the center of the rusty pine needle floor. Charlotte sat cross-legged on one rug and made a sign for Libby to sit, too. Libby's eyes swiveled around the inside of the hut. Birch bark baskets of different shapes and sizes sat stacked along the walls. Some, barely bigger than a fist, held nuts or were heaped with smooth dark red berries. Others, almost as big as laundry baskets, held pine cones.

Libby remembered seeing a pile of curling birch bark strips beside the wigwam. She wondered if Charlotte had made the baskets herself from the pile of bark.

Charlotte sensed her interest. "I come with father. Get bark. Make makak. Fill many makak," she said with pride.

"They're beautiful," Libby said. And they were. "I especially like this one." She held up a birch bark container shaped like the orange juice pitcher her mom had. She ran a finger over the rounded spout.

"Branch grow," Charlotte explained, pointing to the notched spout in the birch bark..

"Cool."

"Cool? Not cool. Warm. From sun." Charlotte looked puzzled.

"I didn't mean cool like in cold. It's just something my friends and I say when we really like something, " Libby tried to explain.

Charlotte frowned. Then she shrugged her shoulders. "Sit. Rest. I bring food. Make welcome?" She smiled shyly.

"Very welcome," Libby replied.

While the Indian girl was gone Libby looked closely at the strange bark walls, the fur rugs, the bark baskets, and wood and bone utensils. She was feeling stranger and stranger.

Charlotte returned in only a few moments. She held out a chunk of flat fried bread and a bowl of some kind of stew. Libby was too hungry to even think about what kind it might be. She discovered it was warm, thick, spicy and very good.

"You like wawashkeschi?" Charlotte fumbled for the English word. "Deer?"

So that's what it was. Deer meat. Venison. "Venison—schmenison," Libby mused. "It's delicious." She rubbed her hand in a circle on her stomach and said, "Mmmm..." to show Charlotte that she liked it.

"What means venison—schmenison?"

"Venison is what people call deer meat back where I live. Schmenison, is just a made-up word. I do that some-times. Just make up words, especially words that rhyme— uh— sound the same," she explained. "Venison-shmenison. Libby-Shibby. Charlotte-Farlotte." She shrugged.

26

Charlotte grinned. "Cool," she said.

Libby laughed. "You know, I think we're going to be friends."

"Yes. Friends. Nniichkiwenh. Friend. Cool," said Charlotte.

Libby tried to say the Ojibwa word for friend, but her tongue seemed to get all bungled up.

Charlotte repeated it slowly, "Nniichkiwenh."

Libby tried again but this time it sounded even worse. They laughed together until a shadow fell across them. Libby looked up to the doorway at the tall silhouette of Charlotte's father that filled the entrance. Her heart began to hammer. She wondered what Marji Gesick would say about finding a strange girl in his wigwam.

Chapter 7

Marji Gesick had to stoop to enter the wigwam. He crouched down on the rug across from Charlotte and Libby. He still wore his red wool jacket and it smelled of smoke from the fire and the pipe the men had been passing around. His face had a hard look, like it had been carved out of bronze rock. It reminded Libby of the faces on Mt. Rushmore in her Social Studies book. He pointed a finger at Libby.

"Anindi wenjibian? Anin ejinikasoian?" he demanded. The words sounded like they were coming from deep down in his chest.

"This is Libby, father," Charlotte answered in English. "She lost in forest. Far away from family."

"Ah." He looked Libby over and while he did she realized that she must look pretty awful - dirty, torn, tired. Then he, too, spoke in English. "Some families not care for girl child. Not like Marji Gesick," he said. He reached out to flip Charlotte's braid, playfully. It made him seem much less fierce.

"She stay, father?"

He nodded. "We go to Kitchi-ogaming. She come. We find Pere, find French traders, find family. It is good you have friend here." He unfolded his large frame, stood, and left the wigwam.

Charlotte smiled fondly after him. "My father love children. Have many children. All die. Only me lives."

"Really?" Libby asked, remembering the times she had wished her brothers might die and she'd be an only child. Well, not really wished it, but.....

"My father have wife. She die. Six babies. All die." She held up all the fingers of her right hand and one from her left. "My mother next wife. Two babies, one boy, one girl - me." She pointed at her own chest. "Brother die. New wife, O-do-no-be-qua. No babies."

It sounded sad to Libby. Sadder than her family's divorce. "I'm sorry about your brother."

Charlotte shrugged. "Many children die."

Libby didn't know any children who had died. She was glad.

"Did your mother die, too?"

"No. Two wife." She held up two fingers.

"Your father has two wives? At the same time?"

"Yes. Father say maybe O-do-no-be-qua have babies. I think she too full of hate for white man. No room for babies inside."

"Why does she hate white men?" Libby asked. Would she hate me, she wondered.

"She say Ojibwa, all People of the Three Fires, sell souls to white men for guns, traps, kettles, cloth, whiskey. She say we sell souls, forget who we are. She angry." Charlotte paused to take a breath, then continued. "See father's red jacket? He trade white man for canoe O-do-no-be-qua make all winter. She much angry. She say she put jacket in fire. So father wear always." She smiled. "O-do-no-be-qua not want father show white men shining rocks. She say they take land. No more hunting ground.

Father say no one can take land. Land belong to all. He say man who shares earth and treasures is great man. Die great man is most best thing. He say it shameful to hide treasures, keep secret. She angry. But he chief."

That seemed to explain it.

Charlotte stretched and yawned. Libby's eyelids were getting heavy.

"Must sleep now. Shining rocks wabang gigijeb - when suns comes."

"Can we go, too?" Libby asked.

" We watch," Charlotte said. She reached into a corner of the wigwam for two soft furs, gave one to Libby and pulled the other over herself as she stretched out on the floor. Libby lay beside her. "Thanks, Charlotte," she whispered. "Goodnight." But the Indian girl seemed to have fallen asleep instantly.

Libby lay there thinking about where she was, how she got there, what she was going to see tomorrow, but mostly about home. Did her mom know what had happened to her? Was she very worried? Libby felt an aching homesickness. She missed her mom, and even her bratty little brothers. She missed Samantha and her other friends in class. She missed Mrs. Maxim. She even missed Nathan Westlake. She squeezed her eyes shut but tears leaked out, rolling over her nose and sliding sideways down her cheek, soaking her hair, before she finally fell into a deep sleep.

Chapter 8

It seemed like Libby had just closed her eyes when she felt a hand gently shaking her shoulders.

"Libby. Morning. Nind ijamin."

What were those strange sounds? Usually Mom said, "Good morning, Sweetie. It's time to rise and shine." Then she would moan and Mom would ruffle her hair.

Libby opened her eyes and looked up into the round smiling face and dark eyes of the Indian girl. At first she was puzzled, but then the fuzziness started to go away and she remembered Charlotte. And where she was.

"Morning?" she asked.

"Yes. Jeba. Nind ijamin. We go soon to shining rocks. Wake. Eat. Father in prayer house. Then go." She handed Libby a broad square of corn bread spread with honey and a bowl of tea.

"Marji Gesick's in a prayer house?" Libby, curiosity aroused, asked between bites.

"Yes. All times. All places. Father build prayer house. He pray spirits help people of three fires. Pray for things people need—animals to come, food to grow, sun, rain. He pray we be brave. Not coward. Not lazy. See?" Charlotte lifted the entrance flap and pointed straight across the clearing to the smallest birch bark hut. It didn't look much bigger than a doghouse to Libby, so small that Libby couldn't imagine how a grown man could fit into it. She could see no door flap.

"How does he get in?" she asked.

"Hole in top. Father go down, up." Charlotte wiggled her fingers down then up, climbing an invisible ladder.

Libby thought it must be very uncomfortable for such a large man to make himself fit into such a small rounded space. "How long does he stay in there?"

Charlotte shrugged her shoulders in what Libby was beginning to see was a characteristic gesture. "Maybe three days. Maybe only little while. Today little while. White men wait to find shining rocks." A frown creased Charlotte's smooth forehead. "He ask spirits for sign."

"Sign? What kind of sign?"

Charlotte stared out over the ripples on the lake, her thoughts far away and troubled. She did not answer and Libby was just getting ready to ask again about the sign when finally she sighed and spoke. "First time in life father not sure," she began. "Father believe it right to share shining rocks. Will give much honor with white men. Promise much white man money. People need. O-do-no-be-qua say no, remind father of legend."

"What legend?" Libby asked, sensing something mysterious.

"Legend of my people. Storyteller say person who show white man to shining rocks will die."

"Really? Does your father believe the legend? Do you?"

Charlotte shrugged again. "One face of father say show white man. Other face say maybe die. So father ask for sign from spirits."

"What about you?"

34

"I not know." Charlotte twisted her hands together and Libby could tell that she was worried that maybe the legend would come true and her father might die. "I think it not true. But...nin gossa—I afraid."

Libby thought about what Mrs. Maxim had said. If Mrs. Maxim was right Marji Gesick wouldn't die until he was an old man, and he would die poor. But not now. Should she tell Charlotte? Would the girl believe her? She wanted to reassure her new friend, but Charlotte would wonder how she could know such a thing. It would lead to questions Libby could not answer. Better not say anything. Instead she put her arm around Charlotte's shoulders. "It's not true." She shook her head confidently. "Don't believe it. I know it's not true." But that was all she could say.

Charlotte gave her a lip-trembling smile and brought her gaze back to the prayer hut.

Chapter 9

Charlotte led Libby to the edge of the lake where gentle waves lapped the sand. She stooped and used her hands to rub water over her face and arms. Libby did the same. The icy water made her think of home and the family bathroom with its soft blue rug to stand on, its sink with warm water pouring out of a silver faucet, and a mirror to see how you looked when you brushed your hair. Today Libby used her fingers to comb through her snarled brown hair.

Back in the hut Charlotte went to a small pile of clothing in a corner and found a long collared vest-like garment that she smoothed out and put on over her long tan dress. The vest had a black background and it was decorated with intricate flower and leaf designs made with hundreds of tiny beads in rainbow colors. At the bottom edges hung fringes of glass beads ending in small, square copper bells. It was the most beautiful thing Libby had ever seen. She reached out a finger and touched a beaded flower, tracing the yellow petals. She ran her fingers through the fringes setting the copper bells tinkling.

"It's beautiful," she said.

"I make," Charlotte replied proudly.

"Cool." Libby said. "Way cool."

Charlotte laughed, delighted. "Important day. Important dress. Important father." She pointed through the open doorway. Marji Gesick stood tall in his red jacket, surrounded by the mining men, speaking and gesturing toward the forest on the other side of the huts.

As she listened to him speak, a question occurred to Libby. "How do you and your father know how to speak English?"

"Fur traders and Pere give us much English."

Libby looked confused. "Pere?"

Charlotte tried again. "Pere. . .father. . ." She brought her right hand up to touch her forehead, her chest and then each shoulder. Then she clasped her hands together like a little kid praying. She repeated, "Pere. . .Father."

"Oh, " Libby said, realizing what she meant. "Priests. Missionaries."

Charlotte nodded. "Much English. Much French."

It was Libby's turn to nod. "Sure. I remember. Father Jaques Marquette was French. There's a statue of him by the Chamber of Commerce in Marquette."

Charlotte creased her brow and looked at Libby strangely. Libby realized that it would be a hundred years in the future before that statue in downtown Marquette would exist.

Just then the men outside began to move purposefully, picking up their packs and equipment.

"We go, " Charlotte said. They left the hut and walked toward the men gathered at the center of the campsite. When Marji Gesick noticed them he stopped and stepped forward. With a few long strides he reached the girls. Then, stooping, resting his hands on his knees, and looking directly into Charlotte's eyes, he said, "No. Daughter not come. Stay." He jabbed a long brown finger toward the ground at Charlotte's feet.

Charlotte began to beg. Libby couldn't understand the Ojibwa words but she was an expert at begging and she could tell by the sound of Charlotte's voice and the pleading look she gave her father that she was begging.

Marji Gesick shook his head. "No! Not want daughter to see. Stay!"

He stood abruptly, turned, and walked away, his red back stiff, so that Libby was the only one to see the hurt in Charlotte's eyes. The girl hung her head.

Libby couldn't stand it. She, too, wanted to see the shining rocks. She wanted to be a witness to the iron ore discovery. She wanted to be the only person who knew for sure if the ore really was found under the roots of a giant pine tree. It had become important to her to be there, to actually know what had happened, to see it with her own eyes.

Charlotte sighed, a deep sad sigh.

"It's not fair," Libby whined. "I came all this way, all these years to see the discovery of iron ore. And now Marji Gesick says we can't come. Why? Why can't we......?" She slapped her hand over her mouth to stop the words that poured out. She hoped Charlotte couldn't understand them all. But apparently she had sensed Libby's anger and understood the word why.

"Father not want me see if. . .if legend come true," she explained.

"But it doesn't!" Libby blurted. "Marji Gesick doesn't die. He lives to be an old man." Oh, oh! Now I've done it, she thought.

Charlotte wrinkled her brows together and squinted her eyes at Libby.

"Just. . .just believe me," Libby implored. "Don't ask me how I know. I just do. You don't have to worry. Honest. Marji Gesick won't die today. He won't die for a long time, many years. I know it."

"You have vision?" Charlotte asked.

"Sort of," Libby said and nodded. Anything to get Charlotte to believe her.

Charlotte's gaze floated away from Libby's face and settled on the group of men just disappearing into the dense forest at the edge of the campground. She didn't have time to think too deeply about what Libby had said. It was time to act. "Must disobey father. We go," she said with quiet determination.

Libby nodded and grinned. "We'll follow them. Stay out of sight. They won't even know we're there. I have lots of practice sneaking up on my brothers. Come on, let's go." She grabbed Charlotte's hand and started off before Charlotte could change her mind.

Chapter 10

In her soft deerskin moccasins Charlotte hardly made a sound. Libby, in her tennis shoes, had to concentrate on setting each foot down quietly. And of course they couldn't talk as they crept through the forest, just barely keeping sight of the group of men up ahead. Libby was glad, for now, that they couldn't talk. How could she answer Charlotte's questions?

Sometimes they lost sight of the men up ahead. But always they could hear the loud voices, the breaking brush, the slashing sounds as the men chopped at limbs and bushes that blocked their way. Libby was glad the men made so much noise because she was finding it hard to be silent. Twigs she didn't know she'd stepped on snapped loudly. Roots reached up and tripped her every chance they got. She made a snake face and hissed at them.

It seemed to Libby that they had walked forever. She wasn't used to that much walking. Usually she got a ride in a car to wherever she was going. Or, if it wasn't far, she rode her bike. She was glad she had worn her comfortable old tennis shoes instead of the new boot-shoes that were so cool looking but pinched her toes. "Shoes-smooz, boots-toots, walking-stalking," she mumbled, wishing the men would stop for a rest. But Marji Gesick led them on.

Finally they did stop. Charlotte and Libby hung back, behind some low bushes where they could watch but be hidden from the men. The woods had thinned in the last hundred feet. Now, instead of tall trees, they saw first low bushes and then the lean grasses of a clearing up ahead. Farther in the distance a rock outcropping that looked like a small mountain edged the clearing. Marji Gesick stopped. A strangled noise came from his throat. He turned around and faced the men, his back to the rock hill.

Behind the concealing bushes Charlotte grabbed Libby's hand. She squeezed hard and Libby could see a worried frown creasing her forehead. In the sun warmed air, Charlotte's fingers felt icy cold on her own hand. She must be thinking about the legend, worrying about whether her father would die. Libby squeezed back on Charlotte's fingers, hard and firm.

Marji Gesick stood with his feet planted, his back to the clearing and the rock outcropping, his face twisted in indecision. The mining men halted and became quiet, watching Marji Gesick warily. Everything was silent, waiting. Only the droning buzz of bees could be heard in the clearing as Marji Gesick wrestled with his beliefs. Finally he took a deep breath. "I not look," he said in a tortured voice. "Spirits of shining rocks not look into Marji Gesick's eyes." Then he began walking backward into the clearing.

Walking slowly and carefully backward Marji Gesick neared the outcropping. The men followed him, still looking puzzled and wary.

At the foot of the steep rocks a giant pine tree lay at an angle. Its bare gray branches like gnarled fingers pointed toward the sky. Half of its roots stuck up in the air. A mound of rocks and dirt, heaved up when the tree fell, lay wedged around the roots, between the tree and the side of the rocky hill. It's true. The fallen tree is not just a legend, Libby thought with a thrill.

Marji Gesick did not move closer toward the fallen tree. He stood statue still. But the mining men spied what lay behind him. They ran forward shouting, the needles of their magnetic instruments dancing wildly in their hands.

"This is it! We've found it! Look at this compass! It's going mad!" They fell on the lumps of rock and dirt, clawing large shiny dark chunks out of the heaved up earth around the tree roots. They held the rocks up to the sun and shiny silver specks gleamed from the surfaces. It looked to Libby like someone had spilled a layer of silver glitter all over the rocks. These rocks looked just like the one she had climbed the monument to touch!

The men threw the shining rocks into the air and caught them again. They laughed. They shouted. They danced. Not Marji Gesick. He continued to stand, still as a carving, his back to the discovery, his shoulders tensed as if at any moment he might be hit with a mighty blow.

Beside Libby, Charlotte stood so still that Libby wasn't sure she was even breathing. Then, still holding onto her hand, she began walking forward, leading Libby to her father's side. She reached out with her other hand and clutched his.

He seemed to come out of his trance. As he looked down at her the granite lines in his face softened into a smile for his beloved daughter. "It is good to share the earth," he said quietly, but there was sadness in his voice.

"Yes, ni papa," Charlotte said softly.

Libby felt a hot lump in her throat that made it hard to swallow.

43

The mining men, still laughing and shouting, began to stuff pieces of the ore into cloth sacks. "What a discovery!" one of them shouted pointing to the rock outcropping. "This here's a mountain of iron!"

Their leader finally noticed Marji Gesick and the two girls standing at the edge of the clearing. In a few long steps he was beside them, clapping a big hand on Marji Gesick's shoulder. "Good work, my man," his voice boomed over the clearing. "We'll take these samples back down to Jackson to be analyzed. If they're as pure as I think they are, we'll start a fine mine on this spot."

Marji Gesick just stared off into the distance as if this commotion had nothing to do with him.

The leader kept on. "We'll honor our promise, chief. You'll get shares in the mine we're going to build here." He waited for a response from Marji Gesick but got none. Finally he shrugged and returned to celebrating with his men.

Marji Gesick took his hand from Charlotte's and moved off, farther away from the pine tree and the outcropping. He sat down on a boulder, still facing away. Libby didn't know what to think. She whispered to Charlotte, "He doesn't seem very happy."

Charlotte nodded. "First time in life he not know what is right thing. White men know how to make things with shining rocks, things our people need. Tools. Knife. Gun. But O-do-no-be-qua say white man change all land and people." She shrugged, not knowing either.

But Libby knew. It made her feel like crying. She knew what would happen to Marji Gesick. And she also knew what happened to the Native Americans and their hunting lands in the next hundred and fifty years. She knew that O-do-no-be-qua was right.

Chapter 11

Their sacks bulged with heavy iron ore rocks. Libby didn't know how the mining men would carry them back to camp, let alone all the way back to Lake Superior. When they were done, the men sat on their full bags. From their pockets they took out strips of dried meat jerky to chew on. They talked about how they would mine the iron ore they'd found, wondered if they'd get rich.

Marji Gesick stayed by himself, standing as tall and still as the trees around him. But as Libby and Charlotte watched he seemed to shake himself free of his trance. He straightened his shoulders and reached inside the neck of his jacket. Up came a long buckskin string. On the end of the string hung an ancient looking dark leather pouch about the size of Libby's clenched fist. He caressed the soft leather with his fingers for a moment. Then he seemed to gather himself up even taller. He took a deep breath and walked purposely forward, frontwards this time, toward the tree roots and the holes left in the earth where the shining rocks had rested. He stood quietly for a moment. Then he began a low chant in what Libby now recognized as the Ojibwa language, full of "j" and "n" and "k" sounds. It almost sounded like some of her rhymes.

Marji Gesick tugged on the buckskin strings, opening

the top of the pouch. Dipping his finger and thumb in, he brought out a pinch of something dark and flaky. It reminded Libby of spices her mom put on homemade pizza. Marji Gesick sprinkled this stuff over the tree roots, the earth, the remaining rocks. He took a few steps to his right. Turning sideways, he faced in another direction and sprinkled more of the stuff . As it sifted down through his fingers he chanted again. Four times he did this, each time facing a different direction.

"What's he doing?" Libby finally asked.

"Father giving sacred tobacco back to earth. Take from earth. Pay back to earth. Thank earth spirit for gifts."

"Oh," Libby said. She thought about Marji Gesick thanking the earth for what they had taken. It seemed to her that he wasn't the only one who should be saying thanks. "The mining men should be giving thanks, too" she said. And maybe all of us who use things made from iron and steel, she thought. "Not just your father."

Charlotte shrugged. "That is way of my people. Is it not way of your people?"

Libby thought about that for a minute. As she thought she began to feel ashamed. She felt shame that it wasn't the way of "her people". Maybe if it were, the world wouldn't be in the mess it was now, she thought. She wasn't sure how to respond to Charlotte's question. Finally she said, "Only some of my people."

Charlotte nodded. But her eyes were now back on her father.

"We go," said Marji Gesick. Without glancing at the mining men he strode out of the clearing and started down the path, toward the camping place. Libby and Charlotte ran to keep up. Behind them they heard the mining men scrambling to lift their heavy sacks and stumble along behind Marji Gesick.

The girls had trouble keeping up with Charlotte's father. The mining men, lugging their heavy sacks, Libby noticed, were falling farther and farther behind.

As she followed Charlotte and her father away from the discovery site Libby began to think about what might happen next. Now that the excitement of the discovery was over new thoughts bothered her. "Charlotte, will we be in trouble? Will your father be mad at us for sneaking away and following them? Will he make me leave?"

"No, I not think he angry. I think he more sure now. Legend did not come true." Charlotte smiled in happy relief.

If Charlotte had been one of Libby's friends from Mrs. Maxim's class Libby knew she would have said, "Told you so." But now she hoped Charlotte had forgotten what she told her.

It didn't seem to take as long to go back to camp as it had seemed when they hiked that morning. Libby didn't know what time it was. All she knew was that she was hungry. She hoped Charlotte was, too. Charlotte walked to a tree behind the huts and unwound a rope that had been wrapped several times around the tree's trunk. She let the rope slide up through her fingers. A bark bag slowly emerged from above. When it hit the ground Charlotte let go of the rope and bent over the bag. She reached in and pulled out pieces of dried meat jerky and fried bread. She handed them to Libby and then dug for more for herself.

Libby looked at the bag, the rope, and then up the tree. "Why do you keep the food up there?" she asked pointing up into the tree branches.

"Keep safe from makwa."

"Makwa? What's makwa?"

For an answer Charlotte rolled her shoulders up, reached her arms up and out and made her fingers into claws. She stepped awkwardly, knees bent, toward Libby and growled loudly.

"Bears?" Libby asked. "Are there bears around here?"

"Yes. Makwa. Bear."

"Bears! I'm scared to death of bears!" Libby wailed.

"Not be scared. Makwa only come if food here for him." She began to pull up on the rope and the bark bag rose high into the tree limbs again. "See? Makwa not come now. No food for him." She patted Libby on the shoulder. "Come. We rest, eat."

Libby and Charlotte brought their food down to the beach. Sitting on the warm soft sand, they ate and watched the sun dance in silver ripples on the surface of the lake. Before long the quiet was broken by the sounds of muttering, groaning and shuffling. They turned to watch the mining men stumble into the campsite. They threw their bags and then themselves down upon the ground to rest.

"Look at their bags," Libby whispered. "They're a lot smaller and lighter than when they started." She and Charlotte giggled. Libby wondered if, like Hansel and Gretel, she could follow the path of dropped shining rocks and find the clearing of the leaning tree again.

Minutes later they heard muffled snoring noises from the men. Libby thought that was funny, too, but she discovered she was too tired to laugh. She leaned over on her side and rested her head on her arm. It was peaceful with the sun warm on her face and the gentle sound of waves lapping against the nearby canoes. She fell asleep.

Chapter 12

The smell of roasting turkey woke Libby from her nap. She sat up, rubbed her eyes, and turned toward the campground. Charlotte crouched beside the campfire, turning a stick that was poked through the carcass of a very large bird. The turning stick rested on two larger sticks pounded into the ground on either side of the fire. Fat from the roasting bird dripped into the low flames making the flames spit and crackle.

Libby walked over to stand beside Charlotte. She had seen wild turkey cooking before on Uncle Bob's barbecue grill. Uncle Bob had let her blow the turkey call whistle he used to lure birds when he hunted them.

"Turkey?" she asked.

Charlotte nodded. "Father hunt. We have feast for finding of shining rocks and riches for all people. Wahang gigijeh - tomorrow morning - we go back to Kitchi Ogaming – Big Lake. Then home to Carp River. Bring you to family." She smiled at Libby.

Libby knew she was supposed to smile back, look happy that they would be taking her to find her home. But she couldn't. Her face felt like it would crack if she tried. Thinking about Uncle Bob had led to other thoughts of home. Lonesomeness washed over her. She missed home, her mom, her brothers, her best friend Samantha, her bedroom, her stuffed animals, her diary, her tooth-brush, her pillow........everything.

A lump the size of a grapefruit and just as sour seemed to fill Libby's throat. She felt tears burning behind her eyes. She fought them back so Charlotte wouldn't see. Abruptly she stood and turned her back to Charlotte. She walked quickly to the beach and plopped down on the cool damp sand. Wrapping her arms around her legs, she rested her head on her knees and let the tears come, dripping down and leaving dark circles of wetness on her jeans.

She had no idea how long she sat in the sand crying before she felt Charlotte's presence beside her. She turned her head and peeked through her hair. Sure enough, the Indian girl had snuck up on her again and was sitting cross-legged beside her. Libby crawled forward on her hands and knees to the water's edge. Cupping her hands, she splashed the cold water on her face. Maybe Charlotte would see that water on her face and not notice the tears.

"Splish-splash, mish-mash," she said, trying to grin at Charlotte. But her lower lip trembled and Charlotte wasn't fooled.

"Why Libby cry?" she asked.

"Cry? Me? I'm not crying," Libby lied.

But Charlotte put her hand gently on Libby's shoulder. "I see," she said. "Libby not happy. Not want to go home?"

"Oh, no, Charlotte! I want to go home more than any-thing in the world. But it's not as easy as you think. You and your father can't take me home. I don't know how to get there."

"Father find," Charlotte said, convinced her father could

do anything. "Not cry. Father find."

"You don't understand," Libby began, sadly. Then she realized that Charlotte couldn't possibly understand because she had never told her the truth. Should she now? Libby debated with herself. She couldn't go to Lake Superior in 1845 with Marji Gesick. She had no home or family there. She couldn't go to his home. She knew from what Charlotte had said that O-do-no-be-qua would not accept her. And how could she explain to them that they couldn't find her family because they wouldn't exist for another hundred and fifty years? No. She couldn't go with them. But what could she do? She couldn't live alone in the forest with the makwa!

Somehow she had to find a way back to her own time, her own home. But how? She had to think. THINK, she told herself pushing on each side of her head with the palms of her hands. She wished she had a smarter brain. Maybe Nathan Westlake's brain could think of something. But she couldn't. All she could do was worry and cry.

Should she tell Charlotte the truth? Could Charlotte help her? Was Mrs. Maxim right when she said that two heads are always better than one? Would Charlotte believe her? How could she?

While all these questions chased themselves around in Libby's brain, Charlotte had sat very still, watching her. Finally she spoke. "I understand," she said. "Something is wrong. Libby want to go home, but cannot. Why?"

Okay, here goes, Libby thought. I have to tell her the truth. How can she help me if I don't? She took a deep breath and blurted it out. "Charlotte, I'm not from 1845. I don't belong here. I'm from the future. I live more than one hundred fifty years in the future. I don't understand it. I don't know what happened or how it happened. I felt strange and then I fainted. When I woke up I was here in the past and you found me at the edge of the campsite last night."

She watched Charlotte's face, fearing her reaction. But Charlotte only looked solemnly at her and nodded slowly. "Yes," she said. "Strange clothes." She ran a finger down the side seam of Libby's jeans. "Strange moccasins." She touched the shoe laces and then the rubber sole of Libby's tennis shoe. "Strange talk. Now I understand."

"You believe me? You don't think I'm crazy?"

Chapter 13

"Crazy - swazy," Charlotte said. She grinned.

Libby's laugh was so quick and unexpected that she snorted through her nose. That set both girls giggling and seemed to break the hopeless gloom Libby had been feeling.

"Thanks, Charlotte. I feel better now. But, do you believe me? Really?"

"Yes," Charlotte said. "I believe spirits do many things people not understand. Spirits of all Anishinabe, people who come before and after, are all around. Spirits watch. Protect Anishinabe. Spirits change. One form, then other. One time, then other. Spirits live in all things, in all ways, in all times. Maybe spirits move Libby." She shrugged her Charlotte shrug. "Many things I not understand. But I believe. I believe Libby."

Libby looked at Charlotte in awe. Who would have thought that Charlotte would believe her, would accept her crazy story as the truth? Libby wondered what would have happened had things been reversed. What if Charlotte had arrived in the future, in Libby's time? Would she believe that story? She didn't know. Probably not at first, but maybe later when she got to know Charlotte. All she knew for sure was that she had never been more glad about anything than she was that the girl believed her. She reached over and squeezed Charlotte's hand. "You are a true friend," she said. As she said the words she realized how true they were. Charlotte had rescued her, befriended her, taken care of her, shared with her, believed her strange story, and would probably help her try to get back home. One small wormy thought of grief wiggled in her mind. If she got her wish and returned home, she would lose her new friend forever.

"Friends help," Charlotte said. "Libby want to go home. I help."

"But I don't know how to get back. I don't know what to do," Libby wailed, feeling hopeless again.

"Tell me all that happened. Then we think," Charlotte said.

So Libby did. She told Charlotte about the stone monument and the shining rock high up that she wanted to touch. "Just like the shining rocks we found today." She told her how Samantha had boosted her up and she had touched the rock. She held up her left hand and showed Charlotte her ring and told her how the sunlight had sparkled on the sapphire and the shiny rock, how the light shot into her eyes almost blinding her, how she had felt a tugging at her body, like a magnetic force pulling her, how she had seemed to disappear into the shining rock that pulled at her, bringing her into darkness, how she woke up lying on the ground in the forest at night, how she followed the firelight down the dark trail to Charlotte and Marji Gesick's campsite.

When she'd finished the story Libby and Charlotte both sat thinking. While she thought, Charlotte twisted the beaded fringes on her vest. The soft tinkling of the tiny copper bells was the only sound for many minutes.

"Can you help me? Do you have any ideas? How do the spirits or the people who travel in time go back and forth?"

"I not know. Spirits bring you here. Spirits must help you go home," Charlotte answered. Then a thoughtful look spread over her face and she smiled confidently. "Must ask Great Spirit for help."

"Pray? Good idea, Charlotte. "

Charlotte raised her eyes to the sky. Libby lowered her eyes. Both girls asked for help, for wisdom, for knowledge of what to do to get Libby back to her own time.

"Now we wait for Great Spirit to answer," Charlotte said. She got up and returned to tending the roasting turkey. Libby just sat still trying to think. Finally Charlotte returned. Her face was alive with an idea. "I think Libby must go backward," she said.

"Backward?" Libby thought it over. Then she grinned and slapped her knee. "That's it! You've got it!" She jumped up, too excited to sit. "It's like when I lose something. Like when I couldn't find my sunglasses. I had to think back about everything I did, everywhere I went, and retrace my steps. Then, voila! There they were." She was talking so fast she didn't know if Charlotte understood it all but she was too excited to slow down.

"That's what I need to do. I need to retrace my steps, try to do everything all over again, the same way, and maybe the same thing will happen again." Libby grabbed Charlotte by both hands and swung her around, dancing and jumping up and down in circles. "Charlotte, you are a genius." she said.

"Genius is cool?"

"Way cool!" Libby assured her and gave her a hug.

Chapter 14

Libby watched as Charlotte went to a low hut near her own. She called and one of the Ojibwa men came out. They held a hurried conversation. Then Charlotte came running back.

"Fighting Bear cook. We go."

"Go where?" Libby asked.

"Backward to future," Charlotte said. The strangeness of the words didn't seem to bother her. "I know trail where Libby come. We follow. Try to find same place." She grabbed Libby's hand and began pulling her toward the forest.

"Wait!" Libby dug her heels in and pulled Charlotte to a halt. "Wait. I have to do everything just the same, don't I?"

Charlotte stood with her hands on her hips, looking impatient. She nodded.

"Okay, then. First think about what we need. I have my ring but we need to have a shiny rock."

"Yes," Charlotte replied. "Need rock."

"We could go back down the trail toward the fallen tree and find the rocks the mining men unloaded from their sacks," Libby suggested, remembering her thoughts about Hansel and Gretel.

Charlotte shook her head. "No. No time." She looked

up, squinting into the sun. "Must find same place while sun is high to shine on ring and rock."

"You're right," Libby said.

Charlotte put her index finger up to tap her bottom lip as she gazed around the campsite. Then her eyes lit upon the sacks thrown into a pile near one of the huts. "Still many rocks in sacks of mining men," she said with a wicked grin. "I think they not count."

"Do you think we can sneak one out without anyone seeing us?"

"Yes. We must. Later, I bring rock back. Come. Quiet." Charlotte slipped quietly around the perimeter of the campsite. Libby followed until they stood at the edge of the forest, as close as they could get to the spot where the mining men had dropped their sacks, yet still stay hidden from view.

It felt to Libby like being a spy on a secret mission as she and Charlotte snuck around, eyes roving furtively in all directions. The only man they saw was Fighting Bear crouched near the fire. From the direction of the beach they could hear muffled voices. Maybe all the men were at the lake. But, Libby worried, maybe some were inside the huts still resting, or listening.

Charlotte pointed to one of the bulky sacks. Libby nodded and they tip-toed forward. When they reached the sack they stopped and watched and listened again. Still no men. No movement.

Charlotte bent over the sack and untwisted the material at the top. She gripped the edges and opened the sack, holding it wide open. Libby reached both hands into the darkness inside. She made a scared mouse face, hoping no snakes had wiggled into the sack of rocks.

She peered in and fumbled around the rocks trying to

find one that was very shiny and not too large and heavy.

"Hurry!" Charlotte whispered frantically, looking over her shoulder. "Men come!" Charlotte had heard them first, but now Libby looked up and saw two mining men come around the side of a nearby hut.

"Hey! What's going on there?" one of them yelled, taking giant steps toward Libby and Charlotte.

"Yikes! Run!" Libby gasped. She grabbed the rock her fingers were touching and hoped it wasn't too heavy. She yanked it out of the sack and took off running. Following Charlotte's bouncing braid and the bright beads and dancing bells of her vest, Libby stumbled into the dense forest.

Moments later, crouched behind a wide tree, panting, they watched the men walk to the sacks and look them over. Giving them a kick, one man said, "Must have been curious."

"Yeah, I guess," replied the other. "Let's go see what smells so good." They headed for the fire, calling to Fighting Bear that the smell of the roasting turkey sure was making them hungry.

"Whew! That was close." Libby breathed out a long breath of relief. She looked around at the dense forest, the huge tall trees, the short bristling bushes, the thick, waist high ferns in all directions. "Can you find the trail from here, Charlotte? Do you know the way?"

Charlotte pointed to the left. "This way. I find."

Libby adjusted her two-handed grip on the shiny rock and followed as Charlotte plowed through the ferns and bushes. Branches slapped at her. She couldn't grab them and push them aside because she needed both hands to carry the heavy rock. When her arms and face had been stung several times by whipping branches, Libby finally thought of a way to free one hand and arm. She called to Charlotte, "Stop a minute."

Charlotte stopped, turned, and noticed the red marks on Libby's arms. "I carry rock," she offered.

"No. I don't want you to get your beautiful vest dirty, or tear any beads off. I'll do it this way." Libby lifted up the hem of her tee shirt and wrapped the rock in the material. She held the rock against her chest, wrapped in the tee shirt, cradled in her left arm the way she used to carry her baby dolls when she was little and played house. Now her right hand was free to fend off the slapping branches. "Okay, let's go."

A few minutes later the girls met the hard packed path.

"You found it!" Libby said. "Now which direction do we go?"

"Go East," Charlotte said. She turned and headed to the right along the trail. Libby no longer had to worry about branches hitting her. But she remembered how she had tripped over roots in the dark so she kept her eyes down watching where she put each foot.

"How far you come?" Charlotte asked.

"I don't know. It was pitch dark. I got tired and it felt like a long long way. But I don't know...."

"Libby watch. See if remember anything. I look for sign," Charlotte said. She slowed her pace, her head swiveling from side to side as she searched for some sign that Libby had walked or fallen there.

Libby couldn't imagine how they would ever find the exact spot again. As they walked farther and farther she began to worry more and more. What if they never found it?

Crash! Libby bumped right into Charlotte's back. "Ow," she said as her head banged Charlotte's and the rock was shoved into her ribs. Charlotte had stopped still in the path. She pointed to the ground on their left. Half hidden under a bush lay a brown paper grocery bag on its side. The red words Econo-Valu looked up at Libby.

"It's my lunch bag! Charlotte, you did it! You found my bag. This must be the place." She looked in wonder from the bag to Charlotte then back to the bag again. "I must have fallen on it and it came with me. In the dark I didn't see it." She knelt and pulled at the bag. "Look. See how it's squished?"

Libby reached in the bag and pulled out her red sweatshirt. She remembered how cold she had been in the dark and how she had wished for her sweatshirt then. But what if she had found it? What if she had put the sweatshirt on, ate the lunch, and taken the bag with her down the trail? They never would have found the exact spot again. "Whew! It's lucky I didn't find it last night," she said.

Next she pulled out a piece of paper with two questions written on it, a squashed peanut butter and jelly sandwich, two oreo cookies, and a small bag of potato chip crumbs.

"Charlotte," she said, grinning, "Forget the turkey. You are going to have a feast from the future now." She took the two sandwich halves out of the baggie and handed one to Charlotte. Taking a big bite out of hers, she began to chew. Charlotte did the same, chewing thoughtfully as she savored the strange new taste.

"It's crunchy peanut butter and strawberry jelly," Libby explained. "My favorite."

Charlotte smiled, took another bite, chewed twice and through the stickiness in her mouth said thickly, "Cool."

Chapter 15

"Okay. Here's what we've got to do. I'll hold on to my bag in this hand. You stand right there, Charlotte. Hold the rock up. Higher. Now move it around until the sun is making it sparkle. That's it. Right there. Perfect.

"Then I'll reach my other hand up and move my ring around until the sun hits it just right and BINGO! I'll be back in the future. I hope."

Libby paused, not ready to raise her hand up yet, though. She knew that the time had come when she had to say good bye to her new friend. If this worked, if she got back home, she'd never see Charlotte again.

"Charlotte," she began. But she didn't know what to say. Charlotte set the rock down. Libby put her arms around the girl and hugged her. "I'll miss you, Charlotte. I'm glad I came. I'm glad I saw the discovery of iron ore. But most of all, I'm glad I met you. I will never forget you. We will be friends through all the future."

Charlotte looked solemnly at Libby. She took one step back. Glancing down and using her right hand, she yanked one of the beaded fringes from the front of her fancy vest. She opened Libby's fingers and placed the fringe in her hand. "To remember," she said.

"Thank you," Libby answered in a hushed voice, closing her fingers over the beads and tiny bell. She tucked the bit of fringe into her jeans pocket. "What can I give you to remember me? I would give you my ring, but I need it to get back. How about my sweatshirt?" She held it up. "Would you like this?"

Charlotte shook her head. "No. Make O-do-no-be-qua angry. I not take anything. Not have to explain anything. I always remember cool friend Libby." She glanced up at the sun. "Do now," she said. She lifted the rock up, arms straining, turning it until the sun shone perfectly on the silvery surface. Libby reached her ring hand up and twisted it until the star sapphire danced in the light. She stared hard at it, holding her breath. She squinted her eyes. She waited. She blinked. She let her breath out. Nothing happened.

Libby's heart sank. Her knees sank. Her arm fell down to her side. She felt like crying. "It's not working," she moaned.

Charlotte brought the heavy rock down and held it, balanced on her hip. "Libby remember every thing? Think. Must remember each thing," Charlotte coaxed.

Libby closed her eyes and tried to replay the whole scene. The monument. Samantha helping her. The spar-kling rocks. The shining ring. The blinding light. The force pulling at her. Mumbling one of her silly rhymes.

"That's it! A rhyme! Charlotte, I just remembered what's missing. I said one of my rhymes just as the light blinded me."

"What is rhyme? What did you say?"

"Oh, my gosh! What was it? What did I say? Oh, gee, I can't remember!" She was hopping up and down franti-cally. "Oh, what did I say? What was it?"

Charlotte's cool hand gripped her arm. "Stop, Libby. Quiet. Let thoughts come." Her soothing voice quieted Libby and she began to search her memory more calmly.

"It was something about Michigan because we were studying Michigan history. Yes, history was in it, too. Let's see........Michigan, wishigan, fishigan, swishigan. Yes! Michigan - swishigan. That's the first part, I think.

"What next?"

"History. History, mystery, twistery. That's it. History - twistory. But there was something else. Just when the light was starting to bother my eyes —something else. Something about sparkling. Sparkling, farkling. No, that's not right. Sparkily? Sparkily - farkily? Sparkily - parkily. That's it. We were at the park - parkily. I've got it, Charlotte. I remember the whole thing."

"Try," Charlotte said, hoisting the rock up high and adjusting it until it shone again in the sunlight.

"This time I know it's going to work. I feel it," Libby said, her veins thrumming with excitement and anticipation. She touched Charlotte's arm. She looked long at her friend, trying to memorize all of her. Her soft brown eyes, her gleaming black braid, her round friendly face, her strong sinewy arms, her tan buckskin dress, her beautiful beaded vest, and her loving smile. "Good bye, Charlotte," she said.

Libby tore her gaze away from her friend and looked up at the shining rock. Reaching, she touched her ring hand to the rock and wiggled it until the sunlight again hit the silvery rock and the sparkling sapphire together. The light stabbed her eyes. She took a big gulp of air. "Michigan - swishigan. History - twistory. Sparkily - parkily," she chanted softly.

Her body seemed to be enveloped by the shining light. It made her whole self tingle. Blinding whiteness surrounded her and she felt herself being pulled by a strong force, pulled into the light. Then a curtain of darkness fell and Libby lost all conscious thought.

Chapter 16

"Ow!" Libby's head hurt. Her back hurt. Her elbows hurt. Her face hurt. Somebody was slapping her cheeks. A voice from far away called her name.

"Libby! Wake up!" The voice came nearer, louder, clearer. "C'mon, Lib, open your eyes."

Libby slowly opened her eyes. She blinked and squinted in the bright sunlight.

"Thank goodness," said Samantha. "I was afraid you were in a coma or something. I yelled for Mrs. Maxim. Here she comes."

Libby sat up. She rubbed the back of her head and shook it gently. "Double ow!" she said. She blinked harder, trying to get rid of the fuzziness. Her eyes began to focus and she saw that it was Samantha kneeling in the grass beside her, not Charlotte. Charlotte, she realized, was gone, left in the past. Libby had made it back to the future, to her own time. In front of her she saw the stone monument rising. Around the side scrambled Mrs. Maxim with a worried look on her face.

"What's the matter? What happened?" she demanded.

Samantha looked at Libby. She didn't want to tattle and get her friend in trouble for climbing on the monument. "Libby fell. She must have tripped or something. I thought she hurt herself. I thought maybe she broke something."

Libby jumped into the conversation quickly. "I'm okay. Just clumsy." She stood and brushed bits of grass off her jeans. She flashed Samantha a grateful smile. Samantha was a true friend, too, just like Charlotte.

"Well, come on then, girls. Most of us have already eaten our lunches. We'll have to get on the bus soon to go to the museum. You'd better hurry," Mrs. Maxim warned as she walked away.

Libby and Samantha sat down on the grass. They used the monument as a backrest. Samantha opened her lunch bag, took out a ham and mustard sandwich, and began to eat. Libby still clutched her squashed Econo-Valu bag by its rolled top.

"Aren't you going to eat?" Samantha asked.

"Lunch - scrunch," Libby said, showing Samantha her flattened bag.

"You can have half of mine," Samantha offered.

"No, thanks. I'm not hungry. I guess falling down knocked the hungry right out of me." She did not want to open her bag and look inside. She did not want to see if her lunch was still in it or not. She didn't want to have to try to explain anything to herself or Samantha right now.

How could she ever explain what had happened? How could Samantha, or anyone else, believe that she had spent a night and a day a hundred and fifty years in the past, when it seemed like only a few minutes had passed here in the present? She was getting dizzy just trying to think about it. She didn't know if she'd ever be able to tell anybody.

"Screeeeee! Screeeeee!" Mrs. Maxim blew her whistle. "Time to go to the museum," she shouted. "Everyone on the bus."

Kids started running toward the bus, trying to get the best seats. For once Libby didn't care where she sat; she absolutely did not feel like running.

As the bus pulled away from the park, Libby leaned her head against the window of the second-to-the-front seat, right behind Trisha's mom. She closed her eyes and tried to concentrate on picturing Charlotte.

"Are you sure you're all right?" Samantha asked.

"Yeah, I'm fine. I just have a bad headache." No wonder I have a headache, Libby thought, my head is so confused. Everything seems so ordinary, like nothing incredible happened. It seems like I fell and Samantha slapped my face a few times and called Mrs. Maxim, and a moment later I opened my eyes and everything was the same as before. Could what I think happened really have happened? Was I really in the past? Or was it just a quick dream? Or a hallucination or something? But it has to be true. It was so real. Night on the forest trail, Marji Gesick and the mining men, the huts by the lake, the fallen tree with the shining rocks around its roots, and most of all, Charlotte.

Her brain was so full of these thoughts as the bus sped to Marquette and the County Historical Museum that she hardly had time to think about the museum. But as they got closer she began to wonder if it would be boring-snoring. But, wait, if it was a historical museum maybe they would have something interesting about the Ojibwa. Maybe even about the discovery of iron ore and Marji Gesick and his daughter Charlotte. She was lost in these thoughts as the bus came to a stop.

Mrs. Maxim and Trisha's mom got out first. They stood at the bottom of the bus steps. Trisha's mom handed everyone a pencil. Mrs. M. handed out sheets of paper that said "Treasure Hunt" on the top.

"C'mon, Libby. This will be fun. We can work together and find all the answers. Maybe we can even beat Nathan Westlake." Samantha pulled Libby along, through the museum door.

"Go up the stairs, class," Mrs. Maxim directed. "The permanent displays are up there. You'll see a life sized diorama of Mr. Burt and his men with their magnetic compasses. There's also a display of early Ojibwas. Look at everything. Read the signs. Listen to the recorded messages. Good luck finding all the answers to the treasure hunt."

When they reached the top of the stairs Samantha wanted to check out all the displays in the order of the questions on the treasure hunt page.

"Uh-uh," Libby said, shaking her head. She could see, off to their right, what appeared to be a birch bark hut just like the one she had spent the night in. "No offense, Samantha, but I'd kind of like to do this by myself, okay?"

Samantha flashed her a questioning look. "You're acting kind of weird," she said. "I think that bump on the head scrambled your brains."

Libby just gave her a large-eyed wise owl look.

"Okay, if that's the way you want it. I bet I'll get all the answers before you." Samantha headed off in another direction. Libby hoped she wasn't mad. But right now all she could think about was exploring the displays from the past — alone.

Chapter 17

Libby was drawn like a magnet to the Ojibwa diorama. As she got closer she could see that there was a hut covered with wide overlapping slabs of birch and cedar bark. A small canoe rested on the sand. Beside the canoe a life sized mannequin of an Ojibwa man dressed in fringed buckskin pants and a burgundy cloth shirt, cleaned a fish. Libby remembered Charlotte's story of O-do-no-be-qua making a canoe all winter and Marji Gesick trading it for his red wool jacket. It made her smile now to remember.

Inside the open-sided hut sat a mannequin of an Ojibwa woman. She wore buckskin clothes with a dark blue calico cape over her shoulders and beads around her neck. In her lap she was making a cattail reed mat like the one on the floor. Beside her rested a cradle board with a baby mannequin strapped in. In front of the baby's happy face hung a dream catcher just like the one Libby had hanging in her bedroom window at home. Lying about were gathering baskets (makuk, Libby reminded herself) filled with blueberries. The sign said this was an Ojibwa family at a working summer camp. It looked so real that Libby once again felt that strange dizzy caught-between-two-worlds feeling.

But just then her eyes lit upon a display case off to the side. The case held tiny intricate baskets and fancy colorful beadwork. She sucked in her breath and exclaimed, "Oh!" Before her eyes hung a beautiful beaded vest. "It's just like Charlotte's," she whispered. She reached out and touched the glass. Her finger traced around a yellow beaded flower. A twining green stem and small pointed leaves led her shaking finger down the vest to the beaded fringe and copper bells along its bottom edge.

"Oh, my gosh!" she exclaimed in whispered awe. Right there, on the right side, in the fringes, there was a gap, a small empty space as if . . . . Could it be?

Libby held her breath. She reached down into her jeans pocket. She felt around until her hand closed upon the beaded string of soft leather. She pulled it out and opened her hand. She held the piece of beaded fringe up to the empty space in the fringe on the vest with shaking fingers. It was a perfect match! She felt a shiver down her back. She clutched the fringe to her chest and let her breath out in one long sigh. Her eyes found the card mounted beside the vest and she read the words, "This beaded stole, worn at times of celebration and ceremony, was made by Charlotte Kawbawgam, well known resident of Marquette County in the late 1800's"

So, it was real. It had actually happened. Charlotte had not only given her a trinket to remember her by, but the proof that she had visited the past.

"Oh, Charlotte - farlotte," she said softly with a smile. She stood there quietly for a few moments. Then she shook the cobwebs of the past from her shoulders and looked down at the treasure hunt paper. She crushed it and shoved it in a garbage can as she went to find the museum worker. She had much more important work to do, questions to ask. She had to start on her own hunt for treasures of information. What had happened to Marji Gesick? But mostly she needed to learn about Charlotte's life. Was she happy? Where did the name Kawbawgum come from? Did she get married? Have babies? Did she live a good, long life?

Libby made a face like a ferret and set out to find some answers.

Libby's Report

Charlotte,
Marji Gesick,
and the Discovery of Iron Ore in
Upper Michigan

a Social Studies/
Language Arts Report
by
Libby Larson

A+

An excellent report, Libby! you make Charlotte "Come Alive"

When iron ore was discovered in Upper Michigan two Native American people played a big part. One was an Ojibwa chief named Marji Gesick. The other one was his thirteen year old daughter named Charlotte.

Mr. Philo M. Everett and some mining explorers came to Marquette County in 1845. They heard that the land here was rich in iron ore. But they didn't know how to find it. They met chief Marji Gesick. He agreed to show them where the iron ore could be found.

It was hard for Marji Gesick to do this. The Ojibwa had a legend. The legend said that if any man showed the shining rocks to white men, he would die. Marji Gesick had to make a hard decision. He believed in sharing the land. He also knew his people could use the knives and tools made from iron. Also, maybe he thought they could get rich. But he had to worry about the legend.

Marji Gesick was a religious man. He prayed to the Great Spirit (Gitchi-Manitou). He decided to take the mining men to the iron ore. This showed he was a man who had faith and courage.

Marji Gesick knew the iron ore was

near his summer camping place at Teal Lake where the town of Negaunee is now. He took his daughter Charlotte with him.

Charlotte was a beautiful girl with a long black braid of hair. She had soft brown eyes and a friendly smile. She could make beautiful baskets and do awesome beadwork. She was very smart. Even though she never went to school she could speak three languages—English, French, and of course, Ojibwa. She also showed bravery when she went with her father even though the legend might come true.

After the discovery of the iron ore the mining men gave Marji Gesick 12 of the 3100 shares of stock in the Jackson Mine they started. Years later it was taken over by the Cleveland Cliffs Iron Company. CCI still has two mines in Marquette County. But the Jackson mine closed a long time ago.

Marji Gesick never got rich. But all his life he kept the paper certificate of his shares of stock. He kept it in a small wooden box with his most precious things. Marji Gesick was pretty old when he died. How old? No one knows for sure because the Ojibwa didn't keep written records at the time when he was born. He died from a white man's disease, typhoid fever. He was in his friend's canoe on his way to see a doctor when he died.

Later his daughter, Charlotte, found his box with his mine shares certificate.

By then Charlotte was grown up. She was the daughter of a chief and she married a chief. His name was Charles Kawbawgum. He is called the last of the Ojibwa chiefs. Charlotte and Charles had two children but they both died. That happened a lot in the old days. But they loved children and wanted to take care of them so they adopted or took foster care of many children.

They lived in a cabin at Presque Isle, just north of the town of Marquette. They were a very popular family in Marquette.

When Charlotte found her father's shares from the mining company she wondered why Marji Gesick and his family never got any money from them. She thought maybe they deserved some profits. So she found a lawyer and went to court. The case went all the way to the Michigan Supreme Court. At the end

Charlotte won the case but never got money. The court said that the original mining men never made a profit either so they had nothing to share with Marji Gesick's family.

Charlotte showed her courage when she fought the mining company for her family's rights.

It seems like Charlotte and her husband Charles had a long and happy life. Charles died on December 28, 1902. No one knows for sure how old he was but people thought he was about 100! Charlotte died two years later.

Using my math I can figure out how old Charlotte was. In 1845 when the iron ore was discovered she was 13. So I took 1904 (the year she died) and subtracted 1845 and got 59. Then I added 13. So she lived to be 72 years old.

I hope she was happy. Someone as beautiful, brave and loving as Charlotte deserved a happy life.

At Presque Isle Park in Marquette there is a large gray boulder that marks the graves of Charlotte and Charles Kawbawgum. If you go there for a hike you can stop and read the sign and remember this beautiful Ojibwa girl.

Photo provided by: Jack Deo

Chief Marji Gesick

Photo provided by: Jack Deo

Charlotte Kawbawgum as a young woman

5

Charles Kawbawgum

Pyramid erected by the Jackson Mine in 1904
to mark the site of Everett's location of ore.

Glossary of Ojibwa words

Anishinabe — the people of the Ojibwa

annin ejinikasoian — How are you called? What is your name?

anindi wenjibian — Where do you come from?

jeba — morning

Kitchi-ogaming — the big lake, Lake Superior

makak — container, basket

makwa — bear

ni — my

nin — I, I am

nind ijamin — we are going

nin gossa — I am afraid, fearful

nniichkiwenh — friend

wabang gigjeb — tomorrow morning, when the sun rises

wawashkeshi — deer

wigwam (or wigiwam) —Native American dwelling made of strips of bark

from: Ojibwa Language Lesson Workbook I & II. published by The Keweenaw Bay Tribal Education Committee, 1979.